Confusing Words

BY
DEBORAH WHITE BROADWATER

COPYRIGHT © 2001 Mark Twain Media, Inc.

ISBN   10-digit: 1-58037-160-4
         13-digit: 978-1-58037-160-5

Printing No. CD-1381

Mark Twain Media, Inc., Publishers
Distributed by Carson-Dellosa Publishing Company, Inc.

Table of Contents

Table of Contents

Introduction

It is important for students, especially today, to be able to communicate with others. This activity book is designed to help students by focusing on a specific skill. Many students do not need all the enrichment activities in this book. The teacher must decide which activities to use to meet the needs of the students. The pages in this book may be used for whole group or individual instruction. Some students may understand the topic after one activity, while others may need more reinforcement.

Teachers are encouraged to copy the pages of this book for use in their classrooms. The exercises will promote the ability to use confusing words correctly in writing and speaking.

Verbs: *Introduction*

There are several pairs of verbs that are often confused when they are used because of similar spelling or pronunciation. It is important to study these verbs to avoid misusing them.

Lie and Lay

Lie means "to recline."

Dad likes to **lie** down on the couch and take a nap after lunch.

Lay means "to place something."

Please **lay** the newspaper on the table when you are finished.

Let and Leave

Let means "to allow" or "to permit."

Did you **let** Stephen use your pencil?

Leave means "to go away."

I have to **leave** for school by eight o'clock.

May and Can

May asks permission.

May I use your pencil for the test?

Can means you are able to do something.

You **can** use my pencil for the rest of the day.

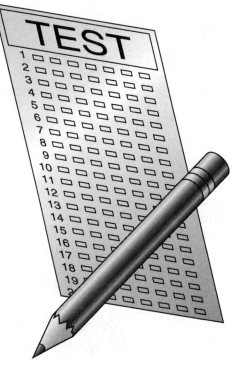

Learn and Teach

Learn means "to gain knowledge."

You should **learn** a foreign language in school.

Teach means "to show how."

It was fun to **teach** my dog to sit up.

Verbs: *Introduction (continued)*

Sit and Set

Sit means "to recline" or "to rest in one place."

Please **sit** at the table and wait for dinner.

Set means "to place something."

I know I **set** my books on the shelf when I came into the room.

Raise and Rise

Raise means "to lift up" or "to cause to go up."

I **raise** my hand when I ask a question in class.

Rise means "to go up by itself."

The bread will **rise** if left in a warm place.

Choose and Chose

Choose (present tense) means "to select or pick something."

Who will you **choose** to be the captain of the team?

Chose is the past tense of *choose*.

I **chose** the red sweater rather than the blue one.

Shown and Shone

Shown is the past tense of *show*.

Were you **shown** to your seat at the play?

Shone is the past tense of *shine*.

The window was polished until it **shone**.

Name: ___Kaitlyn Gilmore_____   Date: ___7-17-10_____

Verbs: *Exercise 1: Lie and Lay*

Directions: Read the following sentences carefully and circle the correct verb.

1. "(**Lie**, Lay) down and take a nap," Mom said to my little sister.

2. Will you (lie, **lay**) the keys to the closet on the counter before you leave?

3. When Sarah comes home, she will (lie, **lay**) her books on the table.

4. Did you (**lie**, lay) on the new couch with your shoes on?

5. After chasing the ball, the dog would (**lie**, lay) under the tree to rest.

6. The toddler would (lie, **lay**) his head on the kitten to feel the soft fur.

7. Bill went to his room to (**lie**, lay) down after football practice.

8. We have 24 chickens, but only six (lie, **lay**) eggs.

9. Where did you (**lie**, lay) your report card?

10. The cat likes to (lie, **lay**) on the windowsill.

11. Are you going to (lie, **lay**) down on the floor or sit up?

12. I can never remember on which side to (**lie**, lay) the fork when setting the table.

13. Where does your dog (**lie**, lay) when it gets hot?

14. I think I will (lie, **lay**) the bouquet for Mrs. Evans on her desk.

15. Please (**lie**, lay) the tests on the table as you leave the room.

Report Card

Math					
Language Arts					
Geography					
History					
Biology					
Art					
Music					
Gym					

Name: Kaitlyn gilmore _____ Date: 7-18-10 _____

Verbs: *Exercise 2: Lie and Lay*

CONFUSING WORDS

Directions: Read the following sentences carefully and circle the correct verb.

Verb	Present	Past	Past Participle
lie	lie	lay	have lain
lay	lay	laid	have laid

1. Plates were (lain, **laid**) on the table at dinner time.

2. The basketball game was so tiring that Ben came home and (lay, **laid**) on his bed to rest.

3. My father likes to (lie, **lay**) down and take a nap after dinner.

4. You shouldn't (**lie,** lay) your muddy boots on the carpet.

5. I (lay, **laid**) the newspaper on the table when I was finished.

6. At two o'clock we will have (**lain,** laid) in the sun a total of three hours.

7. Jeff would have (lain **laid**) in bed all morning if the alarm hadn't gone off.

8. It seems that snow (**lies,** lays) on the ground in Alaska for most of the year.

9. The cow (lay, **laid**) in the country road and blocked the traffic.

10. The two dogs (lay, **laid**) on the porch.

11. "Mom, I (**have lain,** have laid) the keys on the table," I yelled.

12. Do you think I have time to (lie, **lay**) down for a nap?

13. The baby (has lain, **has laid**) in his crib all afternoon.

14. Will you (**lie,** lay) the blankets on the bed?

15. Where did you (lie, **lay**) when you were in your sleeping bag?

Name: __Kaitlyn gilmore__   Date: __7-18-10__

Verbs: *Exercise 3: Let and Leave*

CONFUSING WORDS

Directions: Read the following sentences carefully and circle the correct verb.

1. Did your mom (let, leave) you go to the movie?

2. Will you please (let, leave) me use your new pen?

3. Please (let, leave) your books on your desks when you go to recess.

4. The school bus will (let, leave) at the same time every day.

5. Don't (let, leave) the dog out of the yard.

6. My brother's friends (let, leave) their trucks in the backyard.

7. (Let, Leave) me choose the restaurant this time.

8. Did you (let, leave) your sweater at Jenny's yesterday?

9. How long are you going to (let, leave) your grass grow before you cut it?

10. (Let, Leave) my little brother alone.

11. Will your dad (let, leave) you go to the park with us?

12. (Let, Leave) me alone!

13. Where did you (let, leave) the homework assignment?

14. After school you need to (let, leave) the dog out.

15. I don't think we can (let, leave) Dad alone with the chocolate cake.

Name: Kaitlyn Gilmore

Date: 7-18-10

Verbs: *Exercise 4: Let and Leave*

CONFUSING WORDS

Directions: Read the following sentences carefully and circle the correct verb.

Verb	Present	Past	Past Participle
let	let	let	have let
leave	leave	left	have left

1. Will you (let, leave) me borrow that sweater for the party?

2. Laura has (let, left) her library card expire.

3. Mrs. Brown would (let, leave) us read as many books as we would like.

4. I (let, left) for school at 8:00 to be on time for attendance.

5. Maria has (let, left) her lunch on the bus again.

6. Will you (let, leave) me join your baseball team?

7. Please (let, leave) your bicycle in the bike rack.

8. I have (let, left) a homework assignment on the kitchen table.

9. Caroline will (let, leave) for her trip to Canada in June.

10. Steven (let, left) Jonathan use the computer before the rest of the group.

11. Will you (let, leave) me get my coat before we (let, leave) for the races?

12. Mrs. Yi will not (let, leave) us ride our bikes on her driveway.

13. The boys (let, left) their football equipment at school.

14. Did you (let, leave) the baby bird fly back to the nest?

15. (Let, Leave) me go with you.

6

Name: Kaitlyn Gilmore _____ Date: _____

Verbs: *Exercise 5: May and Can*

CONFUSING WORDS

Directions: Read the following sentences carefully and circle the correct verb.

1. (May, Can) I use the telephone after you?

2. No one (may, can) talk during the speech.

3. Stephanie (may, can) ride a unicycle.

4. You (may, can) be excused from the dinner table after dessert.

5. Juan (may, can) play the violin very well.

6. (May, Can) we please hear a story?

7. (May, Can) a horse run?

8. You (may, can) learn this piano piece if you practice.

9. My sister (may, can) broad jump eight feet.

10. Yes, you (may, can) have seconds on dessert.

11. (May, Can) you do last night's homework?

12. Chris (may, can) play basketball very well.

13. Matt (may, can) go with us to the football game.

14. Birds (may, can) build nests in the spring.

15. (May, Can) you remember the equation for the area of a circle?

7

Name: _____ Date: _____

Verbs: *Exercise 6: Learn and Teach*

Directions: Read the following sentences carefully and circle the correct verb.

1. Could you (learn, teach) me how to play the trumpet?

2. Let Mary (learn, teach) you how to ride a bicycle.

3. New students will (learn, teach) a lot by watching the other students.

4. (Learn, Teach) me a magic trick, Todd.

5. Will we (learn, teach) how to make knots in Scouts?

6. Michael wanted to (learn, teach) how to throw a fastball so he would be a better pitcher.

7. Mr. Meyer is going to (learn, teach) us how to use a drill press.

8. I hope I can (learn, teach) how to do the math problems before the test.

9. Let Kim (learn, teach) us the words to the song.

10. Can you (learn, teach) me how to knit?

11. In history class we will (learn, teach) about the Pilgrims coming to America.

12. People (learn, teach) from the mistakes they have made.

13. Debbie tried to (learn, teach) Kendra how to bake a pie.

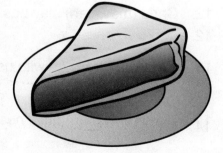

14. Bill will (learn, teach) how to fly-fish from Mr. Potthoff.

15. You must (learn, teach) how to read a map if you are going to travel.

8

Name: _____ Date: _____

Verbs: *Exercise 7: Learn and Teach*

Directions: Read the following sentences carefully and circle the correct verb.

Verb	Present	Past	Past Participle
learn	learn	learned	have learned
teach	teach	taught	have taught

1. Carri (learned, taught) me the words to the new song.

2. Mrs. Weed (learns, teaches) third grade at Prairie School.

3. Reading (learned, taught) Laura about many other places.

4. I have (learned, taught) the piano from Mrs. Elliott.

5. I (learned, taught) my brother how to swim.

6. Mrs. Sanchez (learns, teaches) geometry at the middle school.

7. Miss Garrett enjoyed (learning, teaching) the preschool children how to dance.

8. Your parents (learned, taught) you how to behave at the dinner table.

9. Beth (learned, taught) the class how to use descriptive words in their writing.

10. The students (learned, taught) their spelling words for the test.

11. Mike (has learned, has taught) himself how to juggle.

12. Todd, when will you (learn, teach) me how to drive a car?

13. Curt (has learned, has taught) the dog to fetch.

14. Who will (learn, teach) the Spanish classes next year?

15. Have you (learned, taught) how to balance on one foot yet?

Name: _____ Date: _____

Verbs: *Exercise 8: Sit and Set*

Directions: Read the following sentences carefully and circle the correct verb.

1. Please (sit, set) the packages on the table.

2. I don't want to (sit, set) where I can't see the movie screen.

3. Let's (sit, set) under the tree and watch the clouds.

4. Will you (sit, set) the bookcase over there?

5. Have you (sit, set) the clock for the correct time?

6. I will (sit, set) the pie on the kitchen table to eat later.

7. Did Grandpa (sit, set) his glasses down?

8. (Sit, Set) in the rocking chair and tell me if it is comfortable.

9. We will (sit, set) on the rocks and wait for the others to catch up with us.

10. Hal carefully (sit, set) the goldfish bowl on the shelf.

11. Please (sit, set) on the stool while I trim your hair.

12. I like to (sit, set) up late and read a favorite book.

13. I (sit, set) the vacuum back in the closet when I was finished with it.

14. Mrs. White has (sit, set) a very high standard for our projects.

15. Where do you (sit, set) in the cafeteria?

Name: _____ Date: _____

Verbs: *Exercise 9: Sit and Set*

Directions: Read the following sentences carefully and circle the correct verb.

Verb	Present	Past	Past Participle
sit	sit	sat	have sat
set	set	set	have set

1. The children had not (sat, set) for long before they starting running around the room.

2. The explorer (sat, set) out for the long journey to the New World.

3. Liz (sat, set) patiently while the dentist got his instruments ready.

4. Where are you (sitting, setting)?

5. The jeweler (sat, set) several bracelets on the counter for us to look at.

6. We were (sitting, setting) under the umbrella to stay dry.

7. Patty and I (have sat, have set) the photographs on the shelves in our room.

8. The referee (sat, set) the football on the 20-yard line after the down.

9. Have you ever (sat, set) at the airport and watched the people?

10. My dad (sits, sets) on a special seat when he pilots his plane.

11. My English class had to (sit, set) and wait until the bell rang.

12. The sun was (sitting, setting) in the west.

13. Mr. Macambo (has sat, has set) a dictionary on everyone's desk.

14. Mom (sat, set) the cake down carefully.

15. Will you be (sitting, setting) the boxes in the storeroom?

Name: _____ Date: _____

Verbs: *Exercise 10: Raise and Rise*

Directions: Read the following sentences carefully and circle the correct verb.

1. We will (raise, rise) with the sun to go fishing.

2. In math class we will get a detention if we don't (raise, rise) our hands to talk.

3. The soldiers (raise, rise) the flag every morning and lower it every night.

4. The water level of the lake will (raise, rise) every spring.

5. If you don't keep the bread dough warm, it will never (raise, rise).

6. The weightlifter can (raise, rise) 200 pounds with no effort.

7. Does your temperature (raise, rise) when you have a fever?

8. The sun will (raise, rise) in the east.

9. Will you (raise, rise) your bid on the antique chair?

10. At the beginning of the folk dance, you (raise, rise) your arms up in the air.

11. I think next year I will (raise, rise) tomatoes in my garden.

12. The kite will (raise, rise) in the air with a tug of the string.

13. Our class will (raise, rise) a hamster as a project.

14. Mom is cold, so we must (raise, rise) the temperature in the house.

15. The price of gasoline will (raise, rise) in the summer months.

Name: _____ Date: _____

Verbs: *Exercise 11: Raise and Rise*

Directions: Read the following sentences carefully and circle the correct verb.

Verb	Present	Past	Past Participle
raise	raise	raised	have raised
rise	rise	rose	have risen

1. (Raising, Rising) a pet can be a challenging experience.

2. Mrs. Evans (raised, rose) a question that no one in the class could answer.

3. English people (raise, rise) when the queen comes into a room.

4. When the little boy didn't get any attention, he (raised, rose) his voice.

5. My mom always yells, "(Raise, Rise) and shine," to get us up in the morning.

6. Bill (has raised, has risen) tropical fish for many years.

7. The temperature will (raise, rise) as we get closer to noon.

8. Annie (raised, rose) tomatoes and beans in her garden last year.

9. When the sun (raised, rose) over the trees, the yard became flooded with light.

10. The storm (has raised, has risen) a cloud of dust in the field.

11. The senators (raised, rose) and gave the president a standing ovation.

12. The weatherman (has raised, has risen) the children's hopes of a snow day.

13. You could (raise, rise) your math grade if you would do extra credit.

14. All the pans of bread dough (have raised, have risen) overnight.

15. After (raising, rising) to the office of student council president, Jane moved to a new town.

Name: _____ Date: _____

Verbs: *Exercise 12: Choose and Chose* CONFUSING WORDS

Directions: Read the following sentences carefully and circle the correct verb.

1. Taylor (choose, chose) the brown and white puppy.

2. Which poem will you (choose, chose) to put in the school paper?

3. If I could, I would (choose, chose) Ming for the debating team.

4. Who (choose, chose) ice cream for dessert?

5. I don't know whether to (choose, chose) Spanish or French for a class next year.

6. Do we get to (choose, chose) whom we want on our team?

7. Mrs. Smith said we get to (choose, chose) whom we want to sit next to in math class.

8. Ben (choose, chose) a problem too difficult to demonstrate for the class.

9. If I could pick again, I would (choose, chose) a different color for my bedroom.

10. My brother needs to (choose, chose) a college soon.

11. Please (choose, chose) a slip of paper for the contest drawing.

12. I think I (choose, chose) the wrong shoes to wear in the snow.

13. It is probably a good thing we don't (choose, chose) our brothers and sisters.

14. Sarah was excited that she (choose, chose) to enter the poetry contest.

15. Who do you think they will (choose, chose) to represent the team?

Name: _____ Date: _____

Verbs: *Exercise 13: Shone and Shown*   CONFUSING WORDS

Directions: Read the following sentences carefully and circle the correct verb.

1. They polished the silver until it (shone, shown).

2. The new models of cars will be (shone, shown) at the beginning of September.

3. The moon (shone, shown) brightly in the night sky.

4. On our trip to England, we were (shone, shown) Windsor Castle.

5. Have you (shone, shown) the new students around the building?

6. The plans for the demolition of the library will be (shone, shown) next week.

7. My sister's engagement ring (shone, shown) in the sunlight.

8. The reflection of the stars (shone, shown) in the lake.

9. My history teacher has (shone, shown) more films this year than ever before.

10. Mike's flashlight (shone, shown) on the wall in his bedroom.

11. The dress designer had (shone, shown) the new clothes to her customer.

12. I was (shone, shown) to my seat at the symphony.

13. Have I ever (shone, shown) you my baby pictures?

14. The crystal glasses (shone, shown) after they were washed and dried.

15. I don't think you have ever been (shone, shown) around the city before.

Name: _____ Date: _____

Verbs: *Exercise 14: Review*

Directions: Use the clues below to write the correct verb in the crossword puzzle.

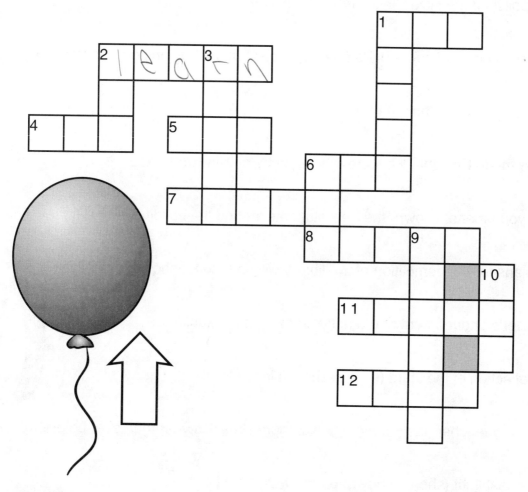

ACROSS

1. To be able to do something
2. To gain knowledge
4. To give permission
5. To rest in one place
6. To recline
7. To go away
8. To show how
11. Past tense of shine
12. To go up

DOWN

1. To select (past tense)
2. To put or place
3. To cause to rise
6. To permit or allow
9. To select
10. To place something

Name: Kaitlyn Gilmore   Date: 7-18-10

Verbs: *Exercise 17: Review*

Directions: Write your own sentences on the following lines, using the listed words.

1. lay _____

_____

2. lie _____

_____

3. let _____

_____

4. leave _____

_____

5. learn _____

_____

6. teach _____

_____

7. may May you bring the baby so I can feed her
dinner and change her pamper

8. can _____

_____

9. sit _____

_____

10. set _____

_____

Name: _____   Date: _____

Verbs: *Exercise 18: Review*

Directions: Write your own sentences on the following lines, using the listed words.

1. raise _____

    _____

2. rise _____

    _____

3. chose _____

    _____

4. choose _____

    _____

5. shown _____

    _____

6. shone _____

    _____

7. learn _____

    _____

8. teach _____

    _____

9. lay _____

    _____

10. lie _____

    _____

Confusing Words

Verbs: *Exercise 19: Review*

Verbs: *Exercise 19: Review*

CONFUSING WORDS

Directions: Match each definition with the correct term. Place the letter of the definition on the line next to the corresponding verb. One definition will be used more than once.

_____ 1. let

_____ 2. leave

_____ 3. learn

_____ 4. teach

_____ 5. may

_____ 6. can

_____ 7. sit

_____ 8. set

_____ 9. raise

_____ 10. rise

_____ 11. chose

_____ 12. choose

_____ 13. shown

_____ 14. shone

_____ 15. lie

_____ 16. lay

A. to place something

B. past tense of shine

C. to recline

D. to pick or select

E. to gain knowledge

F. to allow

G. to go away

H. rest in one place

I. past tense of show

J. ask permission

K. show how

L. to lift up

M. past tense of choose

N. able to do something

O. to go up by itself

Pronouns: *Introduction*

A pronoun is used as the subject in a sentence in place of a noun. It is easy to write the sentence and use the correct pronoun when there is only one pronoun in the sentence.

He went to the ballgame.

I had a sandwich for lunch.

We rode our bicycles to the park.

It becomes more difficult when there are two parts to the subject and one part is a pronoun.

Jim and **her** went to the park together.

Jim and **she** went to the park together.

The second sentence is correct. The best way to decide which pronoun to use is to write or say each part of the sentence separately.

Jim went to the park. **Her** went to the park.

Jim went to the park. **She** went to the park.

The pronouns that are to be used as subjects are **I**, **we**, **you**, **he**, **she**, **it**, and **they**. If the pronoun *I* is used as the subject with a noun or another pronoun, put *I* last.

Jim, John, and **I** went to the game.

Pronouns are also used as objects in a sentence.

Sarah went to the park with **us**.

Carol asked **her** to join the club.

The pronouns that are to be used as objects are **me**, **us**, **you**, **him**, **her**, and **it**.*

*Exception to the rule: Following a verb like *is, was, are,* or *will be,* use **I**, **we**, **you**, **he**, **she**, **it**, or **they**.

The cook is **he**. (He is the cook.)

Pronouns: *Introduction (continued)*

Who and Whom

Who is used as the subject of the sentence, and *whom* is used as an object of either the verb or an object of the preposition if it is in a prepositional phrase.

Who is going to erase the chalkboard? (Subject of the sentence)

The chalkboard will be erased by **whom**? (Object)

To test whether *who* or *whom* is correct, arrange the words in subject, verb, object order.

Who asked the question?

Subject - who   Verb - asked   Object - question

The question was asked by **whom**?

Subject - question   Verb - was asked   Object - whom

23

Name: _____ Date: _____

Pronouns: *Exercise 1: We and Us*

Directions: Read the following sentences carefully and circle the correct pronoun.

1. (We, Us) scouts like to sleep outdoors.

2. Our teacher asked (we, us) girls to collect the books.

3. The pool seemed cold to (we, us) swimmers.

4. (We, Us) six are going to the ballgame after school.

5. The art teacher took (we, us) four artists to the museum.

6. (We, Us) explorers are going on a camping trip.

7. Some friends have been asking (we, us) student council members to plan a school dance.

8. (We, Us) late sleepers are having trouble getting to the bus on time.

9. The mayor will be speaking to (we, us) bike riders about a new bike trail.

10. (We, Us) students are asking for candy machines in the lunchroom.

11. Our ride home from school left without (we, us) three.

12. (We, Us) were elected to the student council from our class.

13. Mr. Meyer said he knew when (we, us) were not ready for the quiz.

14. Mary asked (we, us) to go to the movie with her.

15. (We, Us) will be happy at the end of the school day.

Name: _____ Date: _____

Pronouns: *Exercise 2: We and Us*

Directions: Read the following sentences. If the underlined pronoun in the sentence is correct, write "correct" on the line. If the underlined pronoun is incorrect, write the correct pronoun on the line.

1. <u>Us</u> are going to be late for school if we don't hurry.   _____

2. Jim and <u>us</u> are going out for the football team.   _____

3. Aunt Barb asked <u>us</u> girls to help decorate for the party.   _____

4. <u>We</u> boys rode our bikes to the river.   _____

5. <u>We</u> divers have an afternoon practice next week.   _____

6. The bus driver stopped for <u>we</u> girls.   _____

7. <u>Us</u> girls formed a circle to begin the dance.   _____

8. Do you think the van will hold all of <u>us</u>?   _____

9. <u>We</u> three are going to the library.   _____

10. How do you think <u>we</u> did on the exam?   _____

11. <u>Us</u> four are going to be the first to do our skit.   _____

12. Our principal speaks to <u>us</u> at the assemblies.   _____

13. The dog chased <u>we</u> kids around the house.   _____

14. <u>Us</u> boys are going to the movies at four o'clock.   _____

15. My mom told <u>we</u> five to clean up the kitchen.   _____

25

Name: _____ Date: _____

Pronouns: *Exercise 3: I and Me*

Directions: Read the following sentences carefully and circle the correct pronoun.

1. (I, Me) went to the grocery store with my brother and sister.

2. Janie and (I, me) wrote a song for the class.

3. Carlos and (I, me) should join the debating club.

4. Laura met Beth and (I, me) at the movie theater.

5. (Bill and I, I and Bill) need to study for Mrs. Evans' test.

6. Ling and (I, me) want to go to Hawaii someday.

7. You will go with (I, me).

8. Just between you and (I, me), I don't like hamburgers.

9. Larry almost ran into (I, me) during the game.

10. (You and I, You and me) should sign up for math help.

11. I think that notebook belongs to (I, me).

12. Jeff, Suzanne, and (I, me) are the student council officers.

13. Please pass the sugar to (I, me).

14. Where do you think you and (I, me) should eat dinner?

15. Can you throw the ball to Pat or (I, me)?

Name: _____ Date: _____

Pronouns: *Exercise 4: I and Me*

Directions: Read the following sentences. If the underlined pronoun in the sentence is correct, write "correct" on the line. If the underlined pronoun is incorrect, write the correct pronoun on the line.

1. Louisa and <u>I</u> are going to ride the train to St. Louis next week. _____

2. Where do you think Keeshon and <u>me</u> should ride our bikes? _____

3. Could you hand the paper to Susan and <u>I</u>? _____

4. You and <u>me</u> could eat lunch together. _____

5. Linda, Sherry, and <u>I</u> were ready for the debate. _____

6. When you are finished with that book, <u>I</u> would like to read it. _____

7. Kevin practiced football with Matt and <u>me</u>. _____

8. Wang and <u>me</u> are going to the races. _____

9. <u>I</u>, Susan, and Scott are studying tonight. _____

10. Dad brought Michael and <u>I</u> presents from his trip. _____

11. Andy and <u>me</u> are having a party on Saturday. _____

12. That ball almost hit <u>me</u>. _____

13. Mrs. Martinez gave Brenda and <u>I</u> a ride to school. _____

14. <u>I</u> want to go on a vacation before school starts. _____

15. Jamal, Liz, Matt, and <u>me</u> live in Pennsylvania. _____

Name: _____ Date: _____

Pronouns: *Exercise 5: Who and Whom*

Directions: Read the following sentences carefully and circle the correct pronoun.

1. (Who, Whom) is coming to the birthday party?

2. From (who, whom) did you receive the new book?

3. Do you know (who, whom) will be playing in the football game?

4. Mrs. Evans, (who, whom) teaches English, lives next door to me.

5. The student (who, whom) won the spelling bee last year is going to enter again this year.

6. Carri is the girl (who, whom) I met at the school picnic.

7. Barbara, (who, whom) I greatly respect, spoke to our club.

8. Was it Mr. Mason (who, whom) coached the volleyball team last year?

9. Do you know to (who, whom) the academic award went?

10. To (who, whom) should I address this letter?

11. Michael wondered (who, whom) would be going on the field trip.

12. (Who, Whom) ate all of the candy?

13. Taylor, (who, whom) I was teasing, is my niece.

14. Was George Washington the person (who, whom) crossed the Delaware River?

15. Everyone (who, whom) entered the contest will receive a prize.

Name: _____ Date: _____

Pronouns: *Exercise 6: Who and Whom*

Directions: Read the following sentences carefully and write the correct pronoun (who or whom) in the blanks.

1. I have just figured out _____ the girl in the clown mask is.

2. Did you know _____ Mrs. Weed called on to answer that question?

3. The people with _____ we are visiting are friends of our parents.

4. Can you tell me _____ the first astronauts were?

5. Yen is the student to _____ Mrs. White gave an "A."

6. Curt, _____ is an auctioneer, has a booming voice.

7. We asked Mr. Farmer to _____ he had gone for help with the model car.

8. Bill, _____ had never won anything in his life, won two baby chicks.

9. _____ threw the rock through the window?

10. To _____ do we give our permission slips?

11. Could you ask to _____ they were speaking?

12. It's wonderful that Sarah, _____ is so shy, won the speech contest.

13. _____ will the new art teacher be next year?

14. All day long there were students _____ visited the school.

15. The kids with _____ I was swimming are on my baseball team.

29

Name: _____ Date: _____

Pronouns: *Exercise 7: He and Him; She and Her; They and Them*

Directions: Read the following sentences carefully and circle the correct pronoun.

1. The bus driver gave (they, them) their bus passes.

2. Heather's brother gave (she, her) a ride to school every day.

3. (They, Them) are going sledding after school.

4. Mike and (he, him) will be trying out for the football team next week.

5. I gave (she, her) my notes to study.

6. Jordan and (they, them) have asked for an extra day to study for the test.

7. Did you ask Steve and (he, him) to go to the movie with us?

8. The new students and (they, them) had a tour of the school.

9. Paula and (she, her) rode their bikes to the market.

10. The model airplane was built by Raoul and (he, him).

11. Hal and (he, him) ate dinner at our house.

12. (She, Her) and Betsy baked brownies to sell with the lemonade.

13. The team leaders are Chad and (she, her).

14. The winners were Michael and (he, him).

15. Jackie finally got Laura and (they, them) to sing on key.

Name: _____ Date: _____

Pronouns: *Exercise 8: Review*

Directions: Read the following sentences carefully and circle the correct pronoun.

1. The police officer warned Sean and (he, him) to ride their bikes more cautiously.

2. (She, Her) played basketball with Mr. Carson.

3. Our class officers are Allison and (she, her).

4. I was talking with (they, them) about the posters for the dance.

5. Susan and (I, me) had a great time at the fair.

6. (We, Us) cheerleaders have to practice in the gym.

7. Give (she, her) your sweater to hold while you run the race.

8. The fastest readers are Conchita and (he, him).

9. The carpool almost left without (we, us).

10. (Who, Whom) will be the next principal of the school?

11. (He, Him) will be reading the poem before the whole school.

12. Judy, Pat, and (I, me) are the best relay team.

13. What time are you expecting (they, them) home?

14. On snow days (we, us) like to build snow forts.

15. Alice and (I, me) fixed the flat bike tire.

Name: _____   Date: _____

Pronouns: *Exercise 9: Review*

Directions: Read the following sentences carefully and choose the correct pronoun from the parentheses to write in the blanks.

1. My sister asked Annie and _____ to pull her sled. (I, me)

2. Beth and _____ wrote letters of complaint. (he, him)

3. The last two outs were made by Chris and _____. (she, her)

4. We wanted to see if _____ could play soccer with us. (they, them)

5. _____ are expecting us for dinner at six o'clock. (they, them)

6. _____ and Carl are the best players on the team. (he, him)

7. Debbie and _____ want to bake a cake for dinner. (she, her)

8. _____ boys are going camping on Saturday. (we, us)

9. Rusty, our dog, greeted _____ when we came home from school. (we, us)

10. The bus almost hit Lewis and _____. (I, me)

11. Have you ever seen _____ girls play basketball? (we, us)

12. Will you call Mike and _____ when you are finished studying? (I, me)

13. The goats at the park ate the food _____ offered them. (they, them)

14. Mom and _____ are going shopping for school clothes. (she, her)

15. The leaders of the debate are Stephanie and _____. (he, him)

Name: _____ Date: _____

Pronouns: *Exercise 10: Review*

Directions: Write your own sentences on the lines below, using the listed pronouns.

1. I _____

_____

2. me _____

_____

3. we _____

_____

4. us _____

_____

5. who _____

_____

6. whom _____

_____

7. him _____

_____

8. her _____

_____

9. them _____

_____

10. we and us _____

_____

Homonyms: *Introduction*

CONFUSING WORDS

A **homonym** is a word with the same or similar pronunciation as another word, but it can have a different meaning, origin, or spelling.

Coarse and Course

Coarse means "rough" or "crude."

The sandpaper has a **coarse** surface.

Course is a path, direction, or class.

The sailor set the **course** for Hawaii.

To, Two, and Too

To is a preposition.

I went **to** the store.

Two is a number.

Jane bought **two** apples.

Too means "also."

Jim bought apples **too.**

To is also part of an infinitive.

I like **to** walk in the park.

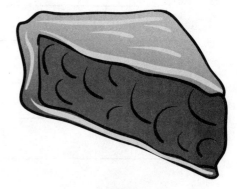

Piece and Peace

Piece means "a part of something."

May I have a **piece** of pie?

Peace means "calm" or "harmony."

The enemies are no longer fighting; they are at **peace.**

Counsel, Council, and Consul

Counsel means "advice."

I got **counsel** from my scout leader.

Council is a group.

I belong to the student **council** at my school.

Consul is a foreign representative.

Mr. Jakar is the **consul** from India.

Homonyms: *Introduction (continued)*

Capital and Capitol

Capital as a noun is a city or town that is the official seat of government of a state.

The **capital** of Illinois is Springfield.

Capital as a noun can also mean "money."

I need **capital** to start my business.

Capital as an adjective means "major" or "important."

That is a **capital** reason for the changes in the weather.

Capitol is a major government building and is usually capitalized.

I visited the **Capitol** in Washington, D.C.

Plane and Plain

Plane is a tool used to smooth wood.

I used a **plane** to smooth the edges of the desk I built.

Plane is also a slang word for an airplane.

The pilot worried when he flew the **plane** in bad weather.

Plane is also a flat, level, and even surface.

A tabletop is an example of a **plane**.

Plain can mean "without decoration."

The Puritans wore **plain** clothing.

Plain can also mean "clearly understood."

It's **plain** that the bad weather is going to make us late for the theater.

Plain can also mean "a flat, level area of land."

The covered wagon traveled across the Kansas **plain**.

Weak and Week

Weak means "not strong."

The cat is too **weak** to raise her head.

Week means "seven days."

School starts in only a **week**.

35

Homonyms: *Introduction (continued)*

Your and You're

> *Your* is a possessive pronoun.
>
> > **Your** mittens are in the closet.
>
> *You're* is a contraction of *you* and *are*.
>
> > **You're** going to be late for school.

Whose and Who's

> *Whose* is a possessive pronoun.
>
> > **Whose** book is on the table?
>
> *Who's* is a contraction of *who* and *is*.
>
> > **Who's** going to be the next person to speak?

Principal and Principle

> *Principal* as an adjective means "the most important."
>
> > Who knows the **principal** exports of Japan?
>
> *Principal* as a noun means "the head of a school."
>
> > Mrs. Jones is the **principal** of our school.
>
> *Principle* means "rule" or "idea."
>
> > A **principle** of freedom is free speech.
>
> *Principle* can also mean "money."
>
> > My savings **principle** grew each year from interest.

Its and It's

> *Its* is a possessive pronoun.   The dog left **its** ball outside.
>
> *It's* is a contraction of *it* and *is*.   **It's** going to rain tonight.

Their, There, and They're

> *Their* is a possessive pronoun.   **Their** bikes were stolen.
>
> *There* is usually an adverb.   You left your hat over **there.**
>
> *They're* is a contraction of *they* and *are*.   **They're** late for school.

Homonyms: *Introduction (continued)*

Stationary and Stationery

Stationary means "unmovable."

That 300-pound slab is **stationary.**

Stationery includes envelopes and paper used to write letters.

I used my new **stationery** to write to Aunt Barb.

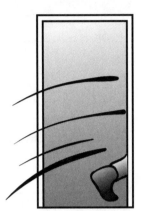

Through and Threw

Through means "to pass from one place to another."

I went **through** the door.

Threw is the past tense of *throw*.

He **threw** the ball over my head.

Break and Brake

Break means "to shatter or destroy."

Did the dish **break** when it fell to the floor?

Brake as a verb means "to slow" or "to stop."

Lee had to **brake** suddenly when the dog ran into the street.

Brake as a noun is a device used to slow or stop a vehicle or machine.

Juanita had to use the **brake** to stop her bicycle.

Cite, Site, and Sight

Cite means "to quote."

Will you **cite** the author for the research paper?

Site is a location.

My dad went to the construction **site.**

Sight as a noun means "the act of seeing" or "something seen."

I had to get glasses because my **sight** was blurred.

Sight as a verb means "to see" or "to take aim."

You should **sight** the castle as we drive over this hill.

Name: _____ Date: _____

Homonyms: *Exercise 1: Coarse and Course* CONFUSING WORDS

Directions: Read the following sentences. In the blank write either coarse or course to make the sentence correct.

1. The sand on the beach is very _____.

2. I took a _____ in geography last year.

3. The race _____ had many hairpin turns.

4. I had to find the right sandpaper, one that wasn't too _____.

5. Of _____, you need to wash your hands before you eat.

6. The old wool blanket felt very _____.

7. My barber said that I have _____ hair.

8. I wanted to take a French _____, but the class was full.

9. The _____ was set as we sailed across the ocean.

10. My grandmother said it was impolite to use _____ language.

11. Do you know what _____ to take for your track run?

12. The rocks at the beach are very _____ and difficult to walk on.

13. I like this relay _____ the best.

14. What _____ of action do you think we should take?

15. This is the most difficult _____ I have ever taken.

Name: _____ Date: _____

Homonyms: *Exercise 2: To, Two, and Too* CONFUSING WORDS

Directions: Read the following sentences carefully and choose the correct homonym (to, two, or too) to write in the blanks.

1. We took _____ weeks to finish our class project.

2. Where are you going _____ buy your new shoes?

3. I asked my sister if I could go to the movie _____.

4. I think I ate _____ much food at the party.

5. I really think my math class this year is _____ hard for me.

6. Rudy went _____ the store with his mom.

7. Kyoko thought there were _____ juice boxes left in the refrigerator.

8. Do you think Mike likes this television program _____?

9. _____ many students are on the tennis team.

10. Pat thinks we need _____ ask permission to go there.

11. This is _____ unbelievable!

12. I need _____ cups of flour for the cookie recipe.

13. Let's wait _____ buy the books until later.

14. My sister whined that she wanted to go _____.

15. The clock read half past _____ o'clock.

Name: _____ Date: _____

Homonyms: *Exercise 3: Piece and Peace* CONFUSING WORDS

Directions: Read the following sentences carefully and choose the correct homonym (piece or peace) to write in the blanks.

1. I would like to have a _____ of chocolate cake.

2. The two fighting nations have finally settled on _____.

3. Could I please have some _____ and quiet?

4. I need another _____ of paper to finish the essay.

5. My baby brother will give you no _____ until you pick him up.

6. Would you like a _____ of apple pie?

7. The United Nations works for _____ among all nations.

8. We need a _____ of paper to make a paper airplane.

9. What can you do with a _____ of string and tape?

10. The dove stands as a symbol of _____.

11. Presidential candidates talk about _____ and prosperity.

12. My grandmother added a _____ of fabric to the quilt she was making.

13. The pie has been cut; may I have a _____?

14. Mom said, "I have not had a moment of _____ all day."

15. Where would you like for me to put this _____ of furniture?

Name: _____ Date: _____

Homonyms: *Exercise 4: Counsel, Council, and Consul*

Directions: Read the following sentences carefully and choose the correct homonym (counsel, council, or consul) to write in the blanks.

1. I hope to be elected to student _____ this year.

2. My dad is a member of the county _____.

3. If you are making an important decision, seek _____ from your parents.

4. Who will be the American _____ to France?

5. Mr. Meyer will _____ the debating team.

6. The city _____ meets on the fourth Thursday.

7. With the help of your _____ I decided to take band.

8. Will the _____ from Mexico meet the president?

9. It is necessary to set up a _____ to help preserve historic buildings.

10. England's _____ to the United Nations is in New York.

11. Did Mrs. Garcia _____ you on what classes to take next year?

12. I have always wanted to be a diplomat and travel as a _____ of the United States.

13. Some people seek _____ when they have problems to solve.

14. Who will we go to for _____ when Mr. Harrison leaves?

15. Our Scout troop will have a _____ to plan our camping trip.

Name: _____ Date: _____

Homonyms: *Exercise 5: Review*

Directions: Write your own sentences on the lines below, using the listed homonyms.

1. coarse _____

   _____

2. course _____

   _____

3. to _____

   _____

4. two _____

   _____

5. too _____

   _____

6. piece _____

   _____

7. peace _____

   _____

8. council _____

   _____

9. consul _____

   _____

10. counsel _____

    _____

Name: _____ Date: _____

Homonyms: *Exercise 6: Capital and Capitol*

Directions: Read the following sentences carefully and choose the correct homonym (capital or capitol) to write in the blanks.

1. On our class trip to Washington, D.C., we will see the _____ building.

2. What is the _____ of Vermont?

3. The _____ of Missouri is Jefferson City.

4. We need _____ if we plan to go traveling.

5. On the map the _____ of a state is marked by a star.

6. All proper nouns begin with a _____ letter.

7. We visited the _____ in Springfield, Illinois.

8. The federal government raises _____ by taxing things.

9. Have you ever seen the _____ dome in Des Moines, Iowa?

10. What was the _____ reason for the start of the Revolutionary War?

11. Does the _____ building in Denver have paintings on the ceiling?

12. Who designed our nation's _____ city, Washington, D.C.?

13. I think buying ice cream is a _____ idea.

14. Bill has always had trouble writing _____ "Z."

15. For the test we need to know the _____ of each of the states.

Name: _____ Date: _____

Homonyms: *Exercise 7: Plane and Plain* CONFUSING WORDS

Directions: Read the following sentences carefully and choose the correct homonym (plane or plain) to write in the blanks.

1. My dad used a _____ to cut down the edges of the doors.

2. We saw an interesting _____ at the air show.

3. The weathered board had a rough _____.

4. Laura Ingalls lived on the Kansas _____ with her family.

5. Carol said it was _____ to her why people liked summer.

6. The cabinetmaker needed a _____ to smooth the tabletop.

7. Grasses grow on the open _____ in the Midwest.

8. The pilot flew the _____ through the thunderstorm.

9. The dress was very _____ without any decorations.

10. The fish broke the _____ of the lake surface.

11. When my dad went to school, there was a class called _____ geometry.

12. The horse ran across the flat _____.

13. The table _____ was smooth and flat.

14. I have been looking for a _____ white sheet of paper.

15. This will be my first trip in a _____.

Name: _____ Date: _____

Homonyms: *Exercise 8: Review*

Directions: Read the following sentences carefully and write the correct homonym from the word bank in the spaces below.

coarse	course	plane	plain	to	two
too	capital	capitol	peace	piece	counsel
council	consul				

1. I need to buy _____ pencils for school.

2. This sweater is very _____ and makes my arms itch.

3. Do you need a _____ to fix the front door?

4. Hal would like to go _____ the movie with us.

5. I have heard the _____ dome is beautiful at night.

6. My mother called this a _____ quilt since it is made up of scraps of fabric.

7. What _____ will the pilot take to get us to England?

8. Will there be rides at the fair _____?

9. I need to borrow a _____ piece of paper for my drawing.

10. There won't be _____ and quiet until my brother takes a nap.

11. On what day will student _____ meet?

12. Who knows what the _____ of Wyoming is?

13. I think the _____ of Italy is coming to speak at our school.

14. If I am confused, I get _____ from my mom.

Name: _____ Date: _____

Homonyms: *Exercise 9: Review*

Directions: Write a homonym for each clue in the crossword puzzle below.

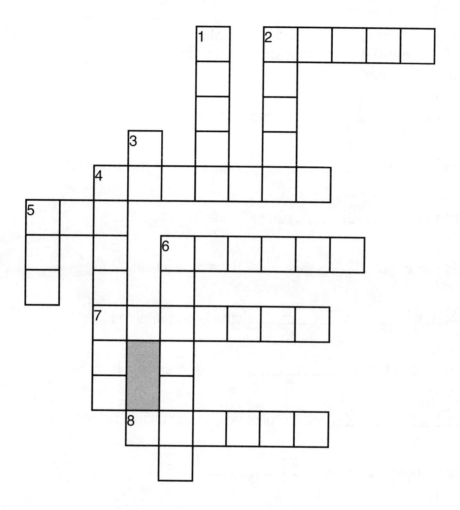

ACROSS

2. Tool used to smooth
4. Advice
5. A number between one and three
6. Rough or crude
7. Major city; adjective meaning important
8. A path or direction

DOWN

1. Without decoration
2. Part of something
3. A preposition
4. A group
5. Also
6. Major government building

Name: _____ Date: _____

Homonyms: *Exercise 10: Weak and Week* CONFUSING WORDS

Directions: Read the following sentences carefully and choose the correct homonym (weak or week) to write in the blanks.

1. This _____ has gone by so slowly.

2. I can drink coffee if it is very _____.

3. I took my film in, and they said it wouldn't be ready for a _____.

4. My birthday is next _____ on Friday.

5. When Sarah had the flu, she felt very _____.

6. For our two-_____ vacation, we are going to the ocean.

7. I have been trying to learn how to roller-skate for a _____ or more.

8. Tim's knees were _____ after he ran the race.

9. What _____ are we going camping?

10. We will have our final exams during the second _____ of January.

11. _____ muscles make it difficult to lift weights.

12. We added water to make a _____ chemical solution.

13. Does the _____ start on Sunday or Monday?

14. Newborn babies have _____ neck muscles.

15. Chris yelled, "See you next _____!"

Name: _____ Date: _____

Homonyms: *Exercise 11: Your and You're* CONFUSING WORDS

Directions: Read the following sentences carefully and choose the correct homonym (your or you're) to write in the blanks.

1. If you work hard, _____ grades will improve.

2. _____ absolutely right!

3. Is that _____ pencil on the floor?

4. Call me if _____ going to the school dance.

5. Are you going to eat _____ french fries?

6. _____ going to be late for school if you don't hurry.

7. I found _____ book about submarines.

8. When _____ reading, make sure to look at each word.

9. Did you leave _____ clothes on the floor again?

10. I don't know when _____ going to finish the project.

11. Could this be _____ umbrella?

12. Mrs. Jones said we could use _____ colored pencils.

13. Do you think _____ qualified to be class president?

14. Luis thinks that _____ hard work will help you go far.

15. _____ the best friend anyone could ask for!

Name: _____ Date: _____

Homonyms: *Exercise 12: Whose and Who's* CONFUSING WORDS

Directions: Read the following sentences carefully and choose the correct homonym (whose or who's) to write in the blanks.

1. _____ papers are those all over the floor?

2. Do you know _____ book report will be first?

3. _____ the captain of our football team?

4. Mr. Brown asked, "_____ the President of the United States?"

5. Dad wants to know _____ dog tore up our trash bag.

6. _____ going with me to the ice cream store?

7. _____ that running down the street?

8. _____ homework has a 100 percent?

9. By what date do you need to know _____ coming to the party?

10. I wish they would tell us _____ going on the school trip.

11. If I could figure out _____ hat this is, I would return it to him.

12. I have always wanted to be in _____ *Who in America.*

13. Can you answer _____ the most important person in the world?

14. _____ books need to be returned to the library?

15. My dad, _____ very tall, played basketball in college.

Name: _____ Date: _____

Homonyms: *Exercise 13: Principal and Principle*

Directions: Read the following sentences carefully and choose the correct homonym (principal or principle) to write in the blanks.

1. I think we are going to have a new _____ at our school next year.

2. _____ Larkin recites the pledge with us each morning.

3. What are the _____ exports of South Africa?

4. Who can suggest one _____ for our student council code?

5. I deposited my _____ in the bank and hope it will gain interest.

6. Raja's _____ complaint is that it is too noisy in the room.

7. The _____ of self-rule came from our forefathers.

8. I think our _____ is a fair disciplinarian.

9. Each of us had to think of one _____ of freedom.

Principal   850.00
Interest   85.00
Total   935.00

10. If you add to the _____, your amount of interest will also grow.

11. Beth's _____ reason for joining the debate club was to gain confidence.

12. What is one guiding _____ that you live by?

13. Do you think the _____ saw us running to class?

14. The _____ of open trade has helped many countries prosper.

15. What is the _____ rule you would like to have changed?

Name: _____ Date: _____

Homonyms: *Exercise 14: Its and It's*

Directions: Read the following sentences carefully and choose the correct homonym (its or it's) to write in the blanks.

1. _____ very noisy at the swimming pool during the summer.

2. I think _____ going to snow tonight.

3. The dog liked _____ new kennel.

4. The morning glory closes _____ blossoms in the afternoon.

5. _____ a touchdown!

6. The cat cleaned _____ paws.

7. George told us _____ time to leave.

8. I can't believe that _____ almost time for school to begin.

9. The dog had _____ tail wagging when it saw the little boy.

10. I love this book; where can I get _____ sequel?

11. Sheneeka thought we should wear our hats if _____ going to be cold.

12. Look at the butterfly; _____ wings look like gold.

13. On Saturday nights _____ fun to pop popcorn.

14. Do you think _____ worth spending all that money on a game?

15. That cat comes with _____ own sleeping blanket.

Name: _____ Date: _____

Homonyms: *Exercise 15: Their, There, and They're*

Directions: Read the following sentences carefully and choose the correct homonym (their, there, or they're) to write in the blanks.

1. _____ asking to go to the picnic with us.

2. Rome is beautiful; I would like to go _____ sometime.

3. I think _____ going to the movie at six o'clock tonight.

4. My sisters hide _____ diaries in the closet.

5. _____ were no raised hands when Mrs. White asked the question.

6. Paul thought we should go _____ after school.

7. We played Polk School in tennis, and _____ team was very good.

8. Students get report cards so they can see how _____ doing in class.

9. _____ very mad because we didn't wait for them at the bus.

10. Do we need to go here or _____ to get our flu shot?

11. Have you seen _____ new puppy?

12. I don't think _____ ready to go to school yet.

13. That's my brother and sister; _____ in the same school.

14. Len could get _____ attention when he yelled.

15. Look, _____ she is across the street.

Name: _____ Date: _____

Homonyms: *Exercise 16: Stationary and Stationery*

Directions: Read the following sentences carefully and choose the correct homonym (stationary or stationery) to write in the blanks.

1. My sister bought new _____ when she went to camp.

2. I like the _____ with the blue stripe at the top.

3. Every day my mom rides her_____ bike.

4. The plane remained _____ while it waited for takeoff instructions.

5. Carri has many different colors of _____.

6. To make sure the car remained _____, a block was put under the tire.

7. I don't think I could stand _____ for longer than three minutes.

8. In business you use plain white _____ for business letters.

9. The flagpole was put in cement to make it _____.

10. Everyone needed to bring a sheet of _____ to write a friendly letter.

11. Tabitha's _____ has her initials on it.

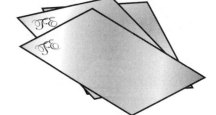

12. The chairs in the auditorium are _____.

13. Those bags of concrete will remain _____ unless we get help to move them.

14. In gymnastics you are to remain _____ after your dismount.

15. _____ is a present my grandmother gives me for my birthday.

Name: _____ Date: _____

Homonyms: *Exercise 17: Through and Threw* CONFUSING WORDS

Directions: Read the following sentences carefully and choose the correct homonym (through or threw) to write in the blanks.

1. Our outfielder _____ the ball from centerfield to home plate.

2. The quarterback _____ three touchdowns in a row.

3. Put the thread _____ the needle.

4. We _____ a tennis ball for the dog to fetch.

5. The large boat went _____ the lock when it went down the river.

6. Can you make it _____ the maze?

7. Phil _____ the paper plates into the trash.

8. Are you _____ with that book yet?

9. The basketball went right _____ the hoop.

10. If you are _____ with your homework, put it in the basket.

11. The baby _____ her spoon down on the floor.

12. To make a potholder, you weave the loops _____ one another.

13. Who _____ the papers all over the floor?

14. He _____ a paper airplane out the window, so he will have to stay after school.

15. We will all be _____ with the play at seven o'clock.

Name: _____ Date: _____

Homonyms: *Exercise 18: Break and Brake* CONFUSING WORDS

Directions: Read the following sentences carefully and choose the correct homonym (break or brake) to write in the blanks.

1. Dad, will you fix the _____ on my old bicycle?

2. When you come to a stop sign, you need to _____.

3. Did the pitcher _____ when it fell?

4. Be careful on the ladder so you don't _____ your leg.

5. I don't wash dishes because I sometimes _____ one.

6. Most cars have an emergency _____.

7. School busses _____ at railroad crossings.

8. If you put your bicycle _____ on too hard, you might skid.

9. The baseball will _____ the window if it hits it.

10. There is a small _____ in the seal of the inner tube, and the air is leaking out.

11. My brother can _____ a toy faster than anyone I know.

12. In the mountains there are signs to remind you a hot _____ will fail.

13. Don't drop the eggs; they will _____.

14. Randy wants to _____ the free throw record.

15. Inspectors make sure there isn't a _____ in the dam.

Homonyms: *Exercise 19: Cite, Site, and Sight*

Directions: Read the following sentences carefully and choose the correct homonym (cite, site, or sight) to write in the blanks.

1. My grandmother's _____ is no longer 20/20.

2. Is your _____ good enough to read that faraway billboard?

3. I think the Indian burial _____ will be an interesting field trip.

4. The waterfall was a beautiful _____.

5. Our teacher said we had to _____ three sources for our research paper.

6. Mr. Matheny can _____ many poems from memory.

7. Did you see the _____ where they are going to build the new school?

8. Bill didn't think the front yard would be a very good _____ for our snow fort.

9. We get our _____ tested every fall at school.

10. Our assignment is to _____ a stanza from our favorite poem.

11. You must _____ the target before releasing the arrow.

12. What is the _____ of the next space launch?

13. Did you _____ the fallen tree he pointed out?

14. There are many types of eyewear that will help your _____.

15. I need to _____ Abraham Lincoln in my Civil War paper.

Name: _____ Date: _____

Homonyms: *Exercise 20: Review*

CONFUSING WORDS

Directions: Read the following sentences carefully and write the correct homonym from the word bank in the spaces below.

weak	**week**	**its**	**it's**	**stationary**	**stationery**
whose	**who's**	**your**	**you're**	**principal**	**principle**
their	**there**	**they're**	**cite**	**site**	**sight**

1. Do you think _____ going to try out for the play?

2. _____ yellow umbrella is in the car?

3. Natalie wears contacts to correct her _____.

4. Sarah got pink flowered _____ as a present.

5. Mrs. Weed, our _____, handed out the awards.

6. Kent and Kim told us _____ dog ran away.

7. Did you _____ the source of your statistics in the report?

8. My knees went _____ when they called my name as a winner.

9. Those flowerpots are so heavy they will be _____ in a tornado.

10. Have you heard _____ trying out for cheerleader?

11. Mrs. Vogel told us to write one _____ of good government.

12. Do we have baseball practice this _____ or next?

13. Look over _____; I think I see a mouse.

14. This is a lovely _____ for a picnic.

15. _____ going to be a long time before we have a school vacation.

16. Is this _____ red pen on the floor?

17. My dog hates to wear _____ coat outside.

18. The boys said _____ not staying to clean up.

Name: _____ Date: _____

Homonyms: *Exercise 21: Review*

Directions: Match each definition with the correct term. Place the letter of the definition on the line next to the corresponding homonym.

_____ 1. weak   A. a major government building

_____ 2. stationary   B. rule or idea

_____ 3. two   C. to quote

_____ 4. capital   D. contraction of *who* and *is*

_____ 5. week   E. not strong

_____ 6. counsel   F. also

_____ 7. site   G. a location

_____ 8. coarse   H. calm and harmony

_____ 9. piece   I. contraction of *you* and *are*

_____ 10. stationery   J. contraction of *it* and *is*

_____ 11. principal   K. paper and envelopes

_____ 12. council   L. head of a school or most important

_____ 13. sight   M. a path, direction, or class

_____ 14. capitol   N. major; important; seat of government

_____ 15. too   O. seven days

_____ 16. they're   P. part of something

_____ 17. who's   Q. advice

_____ 18. peace   R. contraction of *they* and *are*

_____ 19. cite   S. rough or crude

_____ 20. course   T. number between one and three

_____ 21. principle   U. unmovable

_____ 22. you're   V. a group

_____ 23. it's   W. the act of seeing or to see

58

Name: _____ Date: _____

Homonyms: *Exercise 22: Review*

Directions: Write your own sentences on the lines below, using the listed words.

1. capitol _____

_____

2. capital _____

_____

3. plain _____

_____

4. plane _____

_____

5. week _____

_____

6. weak _____

_____

7. stationary _____

_____

8. stationery _____

_____

9. your _____

_____

10. you're _____

_____

Name: _____ Date: _____

Homonyms: *Exercise 23: Review*

Directions: Write your own sentences on the lines below, using the listed words.

1. principal _____

   _____

2. principle _____

   _____

3. who's _____

   _____

4. whose _____

   _____

5. their _____

   _____

6. there _____

   _____

7. they're _____

   _____

8. its _____

   _____

9. it's _____

   _____

10. cite _____

    _____

11. site _____

    _____

12. sight _____

    _____

Other Confusing Words: *Introduction*

Some words are often confusing because they have similar spellings, pronunciations, or meanings. It is important to study these words to avoid misusing them.

All Ready and Already

All ready means "all are prepared" or "completely prepared."

The tennis team was **all ready** to play their match.

Already means "previously."

I have **already** read this book.

All Together and Altogether

All together means "everyone is in one place."

We need to be **all together** before the bus leaves.

Altogether means "entirely" or "completely."

This book is **altogether** too long.

All Right

All right means everything is right. **(Note: You should never write the word *alright*.)**

It was **all right** that you missed two on the paper; it was just practice.

Almost and Most

Almost means "nearly."   A car **almost** hit me yesterday.

Most means "the greatest number or quality."   That is the **most** beautiful bracelet.

Beside and Besides

Beside means "to be next to something."   She put the bread **beside** the toaster.

Besides means "in addition to."   **Besides** Jane, who is going skating?

Clothes and Cloths

Clothes means "apparel."   I don't know which **clothes** to take on the trip.

Cloths are pieces of fabric.   I need some **cloths** to wipe up the water.

61

Other Confusing Words: *Introduction (continued)*

Desert and Dessert

Desert as a noun means "a dry, barren area."

The Painted **Desert** is in the West.

Desert as a noun (often plural) also means "deserved punishment or reward."

For teasing her brother, she received her just **deserts**.

Desert as a verb means "to abandon."

I won't **desert** you in your time of need.

Dessert is a food served at the end of a meal.

Chocolate cake is my favorite **dessert.**

Loose and Lose

Loose means "free" or "not tight."   My dog got **loose** from his leash.

Lose means "to fail or suffer loss."   Did you **lose** the soccer game?

Real and Really

Real means "genuine."   I have a **real** garnet ring.

Really means "extremely."   It was a **really** long movie.

Passed and Past

Passed is the past tense of pass.   We **passed** the car in our truck.

Past means "a time gone by."   My grandpa often thinks about the **past.**

Past can also mean "to go by."   We went **past** the store.

Quiet and Quite

Quiet means "without noise."   The room was **quiet** during the test.

Quite means "entirely" or "to a great extent."   You have **quite** a lot of work to finish.

Than and Then

Than is a conjunction used in comparing.   I like cake better **than** pie.

Then means "when."   First you pour the water, and **then** you stir the batter.

62

Other Confusing Words: *Introduction (continued)*

Good and Well

Good is an adjective and modifies nouns.   That speech sounded **good.**

Well is an adverb and modifies verbs.   I hope I do **well** on the test.

Well is also used as an adjective when describing someone's health or appearance.

Maria didn't feel **well** when she woke up.

Bad and Badly

Bad is an adjective and modifies nouns.   Melanie had a **bad** cold.

Badly is an adverb and modifies verbs.   I know I did **badly** on the math exam.

Accept and Except

Accept means "to receive."   I will **accept** the award for spelling.

Except means "leaving out."   **Except** for Luis, everyone had a part in the play.

Bring and Take

Bring means "move toward the speaker."   Would you **bring** me a glass of water?

Take means "move away from the speaker."   Please **take** your clothes to your room.

Farther and Further

Farther means "a longer physical distance."

Hawaii is **farther** than California.

Further means "in addition to."

If you need **further** help, come in for tutoring.

In and Into

In means "inside a place."   I sat **in** the classroom.

Into means "to move from outside to inside."   Mrs. Jones is walking **into** the office.

Advice and Advise

Advice means "helpful information."   I asked Jane for **advice** about what to wear.

Advise means "to give advice."   Mrs. Bloom will **advise** me on my new schedule.

Name: _____ Date: _____

Other Confusing Words: *Exercise 1: Already and All Ready*

Directions: Read the following sentences carefully and choose the correct word(s) (already or all ready) to write in the blanks.

1. The class was _____ to go on the field trip.

2. What time do you think the scouts will be _____ to break camp?

3. Didn't we do these math problems _____?

4. The students were _____ to leave for the library.

5. I have _____ been to Disney World this year.

6. The moon rocket was _____ for launch.

7. The cheerleaders were _____ for the big football game.

8. Charles has _____ had lunch.

9. Carlos thought Adam had _____ given his speech.

10. David asked if we were _____ to go to the swimming pool.

11. "Let's be _____ when the bus comes," yelled Stephanie.

12. I think Luis has_____ turned in his science project.

13. Have you _____ run your race in the track meet?

14. All right, is everyone _____ for the class picture?

15. The stage manager wanted us _____ when the curtain went up.

Name: _____ Date: _____

Other Confusing Words: *Exercise 2: Altogether and All Together*

Directions: Read the following sentences carefully and choose the correct word(s) (altogether or all together) to write in the blanks.

1. We sang _____ for the concert.

2. Mr. Yamamoto called us _____ to tell us about the accident.

3. This paper is _____ too late to get a passing grade.

4. By putting our heads _____ we came up with the answer to the riddle.

5. Some books have _____ too many characters to keep straight.

6. For school assemblies the grades come _____ in the auditorium.

7. Mom made us go outside because there was _____ too much noise in the house.

8. Do you think we can get _____ and have a car wash next week?

9. Mrs. Rimerez thought she saw us _____ at the movies last Saturday.

10. I think this is _____ too much homework for one day.

11. Look at the triplets sitting _____ on the couch.

12. Please let us go to the ice cream store _____.

13. Your singing was _____ too soft for the audience to hear.

14. Miguel wondered if we could come _____ and make a decision.

15. Mrs. Garrett wanted us to recite the poem _____.

Name: _____ Date: _____

Other Confusing Words: *Exercise 3: Almost and Most*

Directions: Read the following sentences carefully and choose the correct word (almost or most) to write in the blanks.

1. The brownies are _____ done.

   HOME ☐ 6 6
   VISITOR ☐ 6 8

2. _____ of the basketball team are tall.

3. They _____ won the game, but were two points down.

4. Shaquille is so tall he _____ bumped his head on the door.

5. Carol has the _____ brothers and sisters of anyone in my class.

6. Rosy's brother is the _____ handsome boy in the class.

7. Do you have your homework _____ finished?

8. Peter _____ got the rock to skip across the lake.

9. I think this is the _____ homework Mrs. McDonald has ever given.

10. _____ all of the pie was eaten at dinner.

11. My mom is the _____ understanding person in the world.

12. Oh, my gosh, I _____ dropped the cake!

13. Do you think this television program is _____ over?

14. Who has the _____ freckles, Jeff, Amy, or Scott?

15. _____ everyone is finished with the history project.

Name: _____ Date: _____

Other Confusing Words: *Exercise 4: Beside and Besides*

Directions: Read the following sentences carefully and choose the correct word (beside or besides) to write in the blanks.

1. _____ the Tower of London, what did you visit in England?

2. _____ the school building is the park.

3. Mark put the knives _____ the forks on the table.

4. _____ hamburgers, there were chips and lemonade served at the picnic.

5. Do you have any jeans _____ these?

6. Mrs. Stevens wanted Juan to stand _____ Caroline.

7. What are you doing after school _____ homework?

8. Would you put those books _____ the others on the desk?

9. We need to have one more speaker _____ Curt.

10. Does the fishbowl look better _____ the books or the shelf?

11. Do you think others should participate in the debate _____ the student council?

12. Where are you going on vacation _____ Miami?

13. I am training my dog to walk _____ me when we are on the street.

14. I can always count on my brother to stand _____ me when I am in trouble.

15. I think you need to wear something _____ your sweater to keep warm.

Name: _____ Date: _____

Other Confusing Words: *Exercise 5: Clothes and Cloths*

Directions: Read the following sentences carefully and choose the correct word (clothes or cloths) to write in the blanks.

1. During the school year, I really should lay out my _____ the night before.

2. Does your mom let you pick out your own _____?

3. I need some new _____ for dusting.

4. Did you see the _____ we are going to wear for the play?

5. You'll find the cleaning _____ under the sink.

6. Mom has some flannel _____ to wrap the antique dishes in.

7. Yen wants to be a _____ designer when she gets older.

8. Would you get some _____ to clean up the water on the floor?

9. Steve asked for _____ for his birthday.

10. Have you seen the dogs in the circus dressed in baby _____?

11. My dad has special _____ to use when he works on the car.

12. As you study history, you see how _____ have changed over the years.

13. That shop sells _____ for babies and little children.

14. Sports teams have _____ that fans can buy.

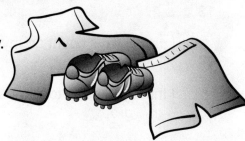

15. Dust _____ always make me sneeze.

68

Other Confusing Words: *Exercise 6: Desert and Dessert*

Directions: Read the following sentences carefully and choose the correct word (desert or dessert) to write in the blanks.

1. My dad loves to have pie for _____.

2. Our camp counselor said she would _____ us in the woods if we didn't behave.

3. Do you have _____ every night at dinner?

4. Ben wished that _____ would be chocolate pudding.

5. What do you think would be his just _____ for breaking the vase?

6. What is the largest _____ in the world?

7. Friends do not _____ friends when they are in trouble.

8. I think all meals should start with _____ instead of ending with it.

9. The _____ has beautiful cactus growing in it.

10. In what country is the Sahara _____?

11. James had a banana for _____, but he wished he had a cupcake.

12. The nomads camped in the _____ at night.

13. Is it hard to find water in the _____?

14. Bill said he always saves room for _____.

15. Being grounded was your just _____ for coming home late from the movie.

Name: _____   Date: _____

Other Confusing Words: *Exercise 7: Loose and Lose*

Directions: Read the following sentences carefully and choose the correct word (loose or lose) to write in the blanks.

1. If the rope is too _____, the newspaper bundle will come apart.

2. I think the _____ belt looks good with your dress.

3. Did the baseball team _____ their last game?

4. Our dog got _____, so we put up signs hoping to find her.

5. These jeans are _____, just the way I like them.

6. My mom can _____ her glasses faster than anyone else I know.

7. Our football team is so far behind, we are sure to _____.

8. That _____ floorboard may make someone trip.

9. I need some _____-leaf paper for Spanish class.

10. Where did you _____ your umbrella?

11. My little brother has a _____ front tooth.

12. I am always careful with my purse so I don't _____ my money.

13. In fairy tales someone always seems to _____ their way in the forest.

14. Make sure the string isn't _____ or your kite will fly away.

15. When did the tennis team last _____ a match?

Name: _____ Date: _____

Other Confusing Words: *Exercise 8: Real and Really*

Directions: Read the following sentences carefully and choose the correct word (real or really) to write in the blanks.

1. The diamond bracelet was _____.

2. Do you think that is a _____ Picasso painting?

3. Rick thought he liked _____ hot food.

4. I had a _____ long walk home from school today.

5. Carol thinks we need a _____ director for the play instead of a student.

6. Doesn't that toy car look just like the _____ one?

7. My dad said he needed a _____ good night's sleep before his meeting.

8. Marilyn was shopping for a _____ beautiful dress for the dance.

9. Annie wanted a _____ rabbit for a gift, but she got a stuffed one instead.

10. Is that a _____ person in the garden, or a scarecrow?

11. The children thought they were _____ scary in their Halloween costumes.

12. Marsha's hair is _____ long; I wonder if she will cut it.

13. It was _____ frightening when the fire truck stopped in front of my house.

14. Those are not _____ flowers in the vase; they are silk.

15. We need a _____ big bag in which to store all the party balloons.

Name: _____ Date: _____

Other Confusing Words: *Exercise 9: Review* CONFUSING WORDS

Directions: Read the following sentences carefully and write the correct word from the word bank in the spaces below. One word will be used more than once.

clothes	**cloths**	**all ready**	**all together**	**altogether**
desert	**dessert**	**most**	**almost**	**loose**
lose	**beside**	**besides**	**real**	**really**
all right				

1. Is the team _____ to get on the bus for the football game?

2. Sammy received her just _____ for studying when she aced the test.

3. The gravel on the driveway was _____, and I lost control of my bike.

4. The _____ is very beautiful at night.

5. Is Susie feeling _____ this morning?

6. Who will be trying out for the lead in the play _____ Tonya?

7. My favorite part of any meal is _____.

8. You are spending _____ too much time playing computer games.

9. My grandmother still has her _____ teeth.

10. I would like each girl to stand _____ a boy for the class picture.

11. Did you pick up all the _____ in your room?

12. I have _____ finished my homework for tomorrow.

13. Did Jim catch the _____ fish on the trip?

14. This puzzle is _____ difficult to complete.

15. I have _____ as many baseball cards as my brother.

16. We put the magazines _____ so they could be recycled.

17. Did your brother _____ you when his friends came along?

18. I hope I didn't _____ my lunch money on the way to school.

19. Where did you put the dust _____ when you were finished with them?

Name: _____ Date: _____

Other Confusing Words: *Exercise 10: Passed and Past*

Directions: Read the following sentences carefully and choose the correct word (passed or past) to write in the blanks.

1. Have you thought about what it would be like to live in the _____?

2. Every day I walk _____ your house on the way to school.

3. I know I have made mistakes in the _____, but I plan to do better.

4. That big truck _____ us going down the hill.

5. Eleven o'clock was way _____ the little boy's bedtime.

6. This year our class is going to study the _____ presidents.

7. This container of milk is _____ its freshness date.

8. Tom _____ by the playground on his bike ride.

9. Do you think you could have had a _____ life?

10. The moon _____ between the earth and the sun to cause an eclipse.

11. We learn from our _____ history.

12. Do you run _____ the grocery store or the library?

13. Look at your _____ test scores to figure your math grade.

14. I would have _____ John in the race, but I tripped and fell.

15. They walked _____ the office on the way to the classroom.

Name: _____ Date: _____

Other Confusing Words: *Exercise 11: Quiet and Quite*

Directions: Read the following sentences carefully and choose the correct word (quiet or quite) to write in the blanks.

1. The room needs to be _____ for the baby to sleep.

2. Our teacher asked us to be _____ while Jim gave his speech.

3. The hurricane we had last year was _____ severe.

4. The television program wasn't _____ over when we had to go to bed.

5. I don't think a toddler can be _____ as a mouse.

6. Do you need the room to be _____ when you study?

7. We hiked _____ a long way through the mountains.

8. The snow has been falling for _____ some time.

9. The Andersons live in a _____ neighborhood.

10. I don't _____ have the music memorized for the recital.

11. The library has posted signs asking you to be _____.

12. Wow, you have grown _____ tall over the summer!

13. My trip to New York was _____ an experience.

14. Liz wished they could keep the barking dog _____.

15. The snow made the woods seem peaceful and _____.

Name: _____ Date: _____

Other Confusing Words: *Exercise 12: Than and Then*

Directions: Read the following sentences carefully and choose the correct word (than or then) to write in the blanks.

1. I laughed and _____ I cried.

2. _____ the door flew open, and the dog came running in.

3. My piece of cake is bigger _____ yours.

4. When you get your books together, _____ we will go to the library.

5. We will go shopping first, and _____ we will go for ice cream.

6. The homework took longer _____ I expected.

7. If I knew what was wrong with the clock, _____ I could fix it.

8. May we open the presents and _____ have birthday cake?

9. Who is better at baseball _____ Lionel?

10. Be sure you put in the eggs and _____ the milk when you make pancakes.

11. The dog is bigger _____ the cat.

12. If you get your room cleaned by two o'clock, _____ we will go to the mall.

13. I think you have more money _____ I have.

14. That movie was better _____ the one we saw last week.

15. Make sure you brush your teeth and _____ go to bed.

Other Confusing Words: *Exercise 13: Good and Well*

Directions: Read the following sentences carefully and choose the correct word (good or well) to write in the blanks.

1. Everyone did _____ in the track meet.

2. How _____ can you draw a bird?

3. The instructions look _____ to me.

4. Our class yearbook turned out _____.

5. Serena's _____ shoes got all wet in the rainstorm.

6. Our soccer team plays together _____.

7. Matt didn't look _____ after his fall down the stairs.

8. My mother cooks _____.

9. The model cars didn't run _____ during the race.

10. Mike told his mom he didn't feel _____.

11. The chocolate cake tastes _____.

12. The plans for the dance sound _____.

13. The choir sang _____ during the performance.

14. The track meet didn't go as _____ as we had hoped; we lost.

15. The chocolate chip cookies smell _____ to me.

Name: _____ Date: _____

Other Confusing Words: *Exercise 14: Bad and Badly*

Directions: Read the following sentences carefully and choose the correct word (bad or badly) to write in the blanks.

1. Our baseball team was _____ beaten in the ninth inning.

2. Six o'clock is a _____ time to have to get up in the morning.

3. Mr. Pitchovski has a _____ temper.

4. My bicycle was _____ dented in the accident.

5. A frown on Mrs. Anderson's face is always a _____ sign.

6. Do you think Steve behaved _____ during lunch?

7. I can't tell if the milk is good or _____.

8. The cake turned out _____ when the oven was set too high.

9. Karen has a _____ cold.

10. Mrs. Martinez said if we were _____ when the substitute was here, we would have detention.

11. I don't think your drawing looks _____.

12. Kevin felt _____ when the carton of milk toppled over.

13. The litter in the park looks _____.

14. You shouldn't treat animals _____.

15. Jim played the piano so _____ the dog would howl.

Name: _____ Date: _____

Other Confusing Words: *Exercise 15: Review*

Directions: Read the following sentences carefully and write the correct word from the word bank in the spaces below. Some words will be used more than once.

bad	**good**	**well**	**badly**	**desert**	**quiet**
quite	**than**	**then**	**passed**	**past**	**dessert**

1. My dog was _____ when she chewed up my mittens.

2. Mitchell plays the piano _____.

3. It was very _____ in the library on Sunday afternoon.

4. My mom baked a creme pie for _____.

5. Sam's punishment for breaking the window was his just _____.

6. In history class we learned about the _____.

7. First we went swimming, and _____ we had a picnic.

8. The other soccer team played _____ in the second period.

9. A huge truck _____ us on the highway.

10. The chocolate brownies looked _____.

11. I think we have _____ a large number of entries for the contest.

12. My brother is a better hockey player _____ I am.

13. Helen didn't feel _____, so she left school for the day.

14. Don't _____ us in the woods; we will get lost.

15. When the white van drove _____ us, it was going very fast.

Name: _____ Date: _____

Other Confusing Words: *Exercise 16: Accept and Except*

Directions: Read the following sentences carefully and choose the correct word (accept or except) in the blanks.

1. Please _____ my apology for being late to the party.

2. Everyone was ready for the test _____ Jason.

3. Carolyn got all the history notes _____ for the day she was absent.

4. I would like to _____ credit for the great idea, but Steve suggested it.

5. Can you _____ Bob from running the race?

6. The swimmers will _____ their ribbons at the end of the meet.

7. Michael thought he could _____ the invitation to go to the movie later.

8. Our homework includes all of the odd problems _____ for number eleven.

9. All of my friends will have lemonade to drink _____ Angela.

10. It will be difficult to _____ having a different math teacher next semester.

11. Do you think the principal will _____ a bouquet of flowers at the assembly?

12. Mrs. Jeffers will _____ the special delivery package for us.

13. Your poster is perfect _____ the time of the dance is wrong.

14. _____ for an hour on Thursday, I have plans every afternoon.

15. Will the CD player _____ this kind of battery, or do we need a different one?

Name: _____ Date: _____

Other Confusing Words: *Exercise 17: Bring and Take*

Directions: Read the following sentences carefully and choose the correct word (bring or take) to write in the blanks.

1. Would you please _____ these papers home to your parents?

2. May I _____ the dog for a walk?

3. I need to _____ my jacket to the ballgame.

4. Please _____ me the newspaper from the living room.

5. _____ your camera when you go to the zoo.

6. Seiji would like to _____ the attendance to the school office.

7. I trained my dog to _____ me his leash.

8. _____ me that pencil.

9. They _____ their clothes to the laundry.

10. If you have the blue book, _____ it to school for me.

11. Marsha will _____ you the letter to read.

12. You can _____ all the football equipment with you.

13. Will you _____ me home after school?

14. I need to _____ a flashlight on the field trip.

15. Carl wished he could _____ his dog to school.

Name: _____ Date: _____

Other Confusing Words: *Exercise 18: Farther and Further*

Directions: Read the following sentences carefully and choose the correct word (farther or further) to write in the blanks.

1. Susan ran _____ in the race than Roger did.

2. I think I can throw the ball _____ if I wind up more.

3. _____ information on that subject is in the book by William White.

4. My dad said we would talk about it _____ when he got home from work.

5. Denver is _____ east than Seattle.

6. My fishing pole is _____ out on the lake than yours.

7. Who rode his bicycle _____, Jim or John?

8. Do you think the room needs to be decorated any _____ for the party?

9. How much _____ do we have to walk before we are there?

10. If we discuss this any _____, I will be late for work.

11. What _____ statistics can we find for this news article?

12. Our gym class ran _____ today than we ever have before.

13. It's warm in here; can that window be opened any _____?

14. Kevin can't reach any _____; he will need the ladder to reach the book.

15. The TV reporter said there will be _____ information on the ten o'clock news.

Name: _____ Date: _____

Other Confusing Words: *Exercise 19: In and Into*

Directions: Read the following sentences carefully and choose the correct word (in or into) to write in the blanks.

1. I jumped _____ the lake.

2. That's Mr. Meyer going _____ the classroom.

3. The balls and bats are _____ the trunk of the car.

4. Many fish swim _____ the ocean.

5. Your sweaters are _____ your bottom drawer.

6. The fans sat _____ the football stadium.

7. Do you think they will let us _____ the movie for half price?

8. My friends and I sat _____ the cafeteria and ate lunch.

9. Ben and his mom waited _____ the car for Steven.

10. Luis dove off the high diving board _____ the pool.

11. Matt lost his key, so he couldn't get _____ his house.

12. Where will your science display be _____ the gymnasium?

13. Phil's hand would not fit _____ the glove.

14. Look, Mike and Will are getting _____ Mrs. Johnson's car.

15. You'll find the cookies _____ the pantry.

Name: _____ Date: _____

Other Confusing Words: *Exercise 20: Advice and Advise*

Directions: Read the following sentences carefully and choose the correct word (advice or advise) to write in the blanks.

1. Hank asked Rupert for _____ on how to repair his bicycle.

2. There are people who write _____ columns in the newspapers.

3. Mrs. Fujimori will _____ us on what to do in student council.

4. Sometimes when you have a problem, you don't want a lot of _____.

5. Could you _____ me on the best route to get to the park?

6. Mrs. Elliot said, "I _____ you to practice the piano more often."

7. People always like to give _____, but often don't like to take it.

8. Are you going to listen to the _____ Mr. Garcia gave about basketball?

9. Paula wanted to find someone to _____ her on which contest to enter.

10. Where do you think parents go for _____?

11. Our counselors _____ us on which classes to take each year.

12. I would _____ you to put a light on your bike if you will be riding in the dark.

13. If you could give a younger student one piece of _____, what would you say?

14. Brenda thought that, for once, Kim's _____ was correct.

15. People often don't like to hear others' _____.

Name: _____ Date: _____

Other Confusing Words: *Exercise 21: Review*

Directions: Read the following sentences carefully and write the correct word from the word bank in the spaces below. Some words will be used more than once.

advice	in	accept	advise	farther
further	into	bring	except	take

1. It was so hot, we dove right _____ the pool.

2. "I would _____ you to clean up your room," Mother said.

3. Paul needs to _____ his library books back to the library.

4. Your paper airplane flew _____ than mine.

5. Do I need to _____ anything to the party?

6. Would you please _____ this award?

7. I have everyone's project _____ Stephanie's.

8. Our summer trip took us _____ than Bobby's.

9. Scott is sitting _____ the library.

10. My _____ is to fence your yard if you have a dog.

11. May I _____ the dog inside the house?

12. Our car rolled right _____ the garage door.

13. Would you _____ explain problem 27?

14. How long have you been _____ this classroom?

Name: _____ Date: _____

Other Confusing Words: *Exercise 22: Review*

Directions: Match each definition with the correct term. Place the letter of the definition on the line next to the corresponding word.

_____ 1. advice

_____ 2. passed

_____ 3. then

_____ 4. in

_____ 5. farther

_____ 6. quite

_____ 7. advise

_____ 8. good

_____ 9. badly

_____ 10. quiet

_____ 11. past

_____ 12. than

_____ 13. into

_____ 14. bring

_____ 15. further

_____ 16. accept

_____ 17. well

_____ 18. take

_____ 19. except

_____ 20. bad

A. an adjective (positive)

B. a time gone by

C. to give advice

D. leaving out

E. in addition to

F. when

G. past tense of pass

H. to receive

I. helpful information

J. a longer physical distance

K. to a great extent

L. an adjective (negative)

M. used to describe someone's health

N. without noise

O. adverb (negative)

P. conjunction used for comparing

Q. toward the speaker

R. move from outside to inside

S. inside a place

T. away from the speaker

Name: _____ Date: _____

Other Confusing Words: *Exercise 23: Review* CONFUSING WORDS

Directions: Write your own sentences on the following lines, using the listed words.

1. in _____

_____

2. into _____

_____

3. accept _____

_____

4. except _____

_____

5. bring _____

_____

6. take _____

_____

7. advice _____

_____

8. advise _____

_____

9. farther _____

_____

10. further _____

_____

Name: _____ Date: _____

Other Confusing Words: *Exercise 24: Review*

Directions: Keep your own list of confusing words on this sheet. Write the word and then look up the definition in the dictionary.

Word	Definition
_____	_____
_____	_____
_____	_____
_____	_____
_____	_____
_____	_____
_____	_____
_____	_____
_____	_____
_____	_____
_____	_____
_____	_____
_____	_____
_____	_____
_____	_____
_____	_____
_____	_____
_____	_____
_____	_____

Answer Keys

CONFUSING WORDS

Verbs: Exercise 1:
Lie and Lay (p. 3)
1. Lie
2. lay
3. lay
4. lie
5. lie
6. lay
7. lie
8. lay
9. lay
10. lie
11. lie
12. lay
13. lie
14. lay
15. lay

Verbs: Exercise 2:
Lie and Lay (p. 4)
1. laid
2. lay
3. lie
4. lay
5. laid
6. lain
7. lain
8. lies
9. lay
10. lay
11. have laid
12. lie
13. has lain
14. lay
15. lie

Verbs: Exercise 3:
Let and Leave (p. 5)
1. let
2. let
3. leave
4. leave
5. let
6. leave
7. Let
8. leave
9. let
10. Leave
11. let
12. Leave
13. leave

14. let
15. leave

Verbs: Exercise 4:
Let and Leave (p. 6)
1. let
2. let
3. let
4. left
5. left
6. let
7. leave
8. left
9. leave
10. let
11. let, leave
12. let
13. left
14. let
15. Let

Verbs: Exercise 5:
May and Can (p. 7)
1. May
2. may
3. can
4. may
5. can
6. May
7. Can
8. can
9. can
10. may
11. Can
12. can
13. may
14. can
15. Can

Verbs: Exercise 6:
Learn and Teach
(p. 8)
1. teach
2. teach
3. learn
4. Teach
5. learn
6. learn
7. teach
8. learn
9. teach

10. teach
11. learn
12. learn
13. teach
14. learn
15. learn

Verbs: Exercise 7:
Learn and Teach
(p. 9)
1. taught
2. teaches
3. taught
4. learned
5. taught
6. teaches
7. teaching
8. taught
9. taught
10. learned
11. has taught
12. teach
13. has taught
14. teach
15. learned

Verbs: Exercise 8:
Sit and Set (p. 10)
1. set
2. sit
3. sit
4. set
5. set
6. set
7. set
8. Sit
9. sit
10. set
11. sit
12. sit
13. set
14. set
15. sit

Verbs: Exercise 9:
Sit and Set (p. 11)
1. sat
2. set
3. sat
4. sitting
5. set

6. sitting
7. have set
8. set
9. sat
10. sits
11. sit
12. setting
13. has set
14. set
15. setting

Verbs: Exercise 10:
Raise and Rise
(p. 12)
1. rise
2. raise
3. raise
4. rise
5. rise
6. raise
7. rise
8. rise
9. raise
10. raise
11. raise
12. rise
13. raise
14. raise
15. rise

Verbs: Exercise 11:
Raise and Rise
(p. 13)
1. Raising
2. raised
3. rise
4. raised
5. Rise
6. has raised
7. rise
8. raised
9. rose
10. has raised
11. rose
12. has raised
13. raise
14. have risen
15. rising

Verbs: Exercise 12:
Choose and Chose
(p. 14)
1. chose
2. choose
3. choose
4. chose
5. choose
6. choose
7. choose
8. chose
9. choose
10. choose
11. choose
12. chose
13. choose
14. chose
15. choose

Verbs: Exercise 13:
Shone and Shown
(p. 15)
1. shone
2. shown
3. shone
4. shown
5. shown
6. shown
7. shone
8. shone
9. shown
10. shone
11. shown
12. shown
13. shown
14. shone
15. shown

Verbs: Exercise 14:
Review (p. 16)

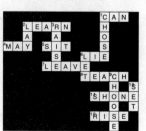

Verbs: Exercise 15: Review (p. 17)
1. raise
2. lay
3. rise
4. lie
5. teach
6. shone
7. set
8. sit
9. choose
10. learned
11. left
12. chose
13. let
14. shown
15. may
16. can

Verbs: Exercise 16: Review (p. 18)
1. have raised
2. set
3. sit
4. taught
5. rise
6. laid
7. lay
8. learned
9. has let
10. set
11. rose
12. left
13. sat
14. raised
15. teach

Verbs: Exercise 19: Review (p. 21)
1. F
2. G
3. E
4. K
5. J
6. N
7. H
8. A
9. L
10. O
11. M
12. D
13. I
14. B
15. C
16. A

Pronouns: Exercise 1: We and Us (p. 24)
1. We
2. us
3. us
4. We
5. us
6. We
7. us
8. We
9. us
10. We
11. us
12. We
13. we
14. us
15. We

Pronouns: Exercise 2: We and Us (p. 25)
1. incorrect - We
2. incorrect - we
3. correct
4. correct
5. correct
6. incorrect - us
7. incorrect - We
8. correct
9. correct
10. correct
11. incorrect - We
12. correct
13. incorrect - us
14. incorrect - We
15. incorrect - us

Pronouns: Exercise 3: I and Me (p. 26)
1. I
2. I
3. I
4. me
5. Bill and I
6. I
7. me
8. me
9. me
10. You and I
11. me
12. I
13. me
14. I
15. me

Pronouns: Exercise 4: I and Me (p. 27)
1. correct
2. incorrect - I
3. incorrect - me
4. incorrect - I
5. correct
6. correct
7. correct
8. incorrect - I
9. incorrect - Susan, Scott, and I
10. incorrect - me
11. incorrect - I
12. correct
13. incorrect - me
14. correct
15. incorrect - I

Pronouns: Exercise 5: Who and Whom (p. 28)
1. Who
2. whom
3. whom
4. who
5. who
6. whom
7. whom
8. who
9. whom
10. whom
11. who
12. Who
13. whom
14. who
15. who

Pronouns: Exercise 6: Who and Whom (p. 29)
1. whom
2. whom
3. whom
4. who
5. whom
6. who
7. whom
8. who
9. Who
10. whom
11. whom
12. who
13. Whom
14. who
15. whom

Pronouns: Exercise 7: He and Him; She and Her; They and Them (p. 30)
1. them
2. her
3. They
4. he
5. her
6. they
7. him
8. they
9. she
10. him
11. he
12. She
13. she
14. he
15. them

Pronouns: Exercise 8: Review (p. 31)
1. him
2. She
3. she
4. them
5. I
6. We
7. her
8. he
9. us
10. Who
11. He
12. I
13. them
14. we
15. I

Pronouns: Exercise 9: Review (p. 32)
1. me
2. he
3. her
4. they
5. They
6. He
7. she
8. We
9. us
10. me
11. us
12. me
13. they
14. she
15. he

Homonyms: Exercise 1: Coarse and Course (p. 38)
1. coarse
2. course
3. course
4. coarse
5. course
6. coarse
7. coarse
8. course
9. course
10. coarse
11. course
12. coarse
13. course
14. course
15. course

Homonyms: Exercise 2: To, Two, and Too (p. 39)
1. two
2. to
3. too
4. too
5. too
6. to
7. two
8. too
9. Too
10. to
11. too
12. two
13. to
14. too
15. two

**Homonyms:
Exercise 3:
Piece and Peace
(p. 40)**
1. piece
2. peace
3. peace
4. piece
5. peace
6. piece
7. peace
8. piece
9. piece
10. peace
11. peace
12. piece
13. piece
14. peace
15. piece

**Homonyms:
Exercise 4:
Counsel, Council,
and Consul (p. 41)**
1. council
2. council
3. counsel
4. consul
5. counsel
6. council
7. counsel
8. consul
9. council
10. consul
11. counsel
12. consul
13. counsel
14. counsel
15. council

**Homonyms:
Exercise 6:
Capital and Capitol
(p. 43)**
1. Capitol
2. capital
3. capital
4. capital
5. capital
6. capital
7. capitol
8. capital
9. capitol
10. capital
11. capitol

12. capital
13. capital
14. capital
15. capital

**Homonyms:
Exercise 7:
Plane and Plain
(p. 44)**
1. plane
2. plane
3. plane
4. plain
5. plain
6. plane
7. plain
8. plane
9. plain
10. plane
11. plane
12. plain
13. plane
14. plain
15. plane

**Homonyms:
Exercise 8:
Review (p. 45)**
1. two
2. coarse
3. plane
4. to
5. capitol
6. piece
7. course
8. too
9. plain
10. peace
11. council
12. capital
13. consul
14. counsel

**Homonyms:
Exercise 9:
Review (p. 46)**

**Homonyms:
Exercise 10:
Weak and Week
(p. 47)**
1. week
2. weak
3. week
4. week
5. weak
6. week
7. week
8. weak
9. week
10. week
11. Weak
12. weak
13. week
14. weak
15. week

**Homonyms:
Exercise 11:
Your and You're
(p. 48)**
1. your
2. You're
3. your
4. you're
5. your
6. You're
7. your
8. you're
9. your
10. you're
11. your
12. your
13. you're
14. your
15. You're

**Homonyms:
Exercise 12:
Whose and Who's
(p. 49)**
1. Whose
2. whose
3. Who's
4. Who's
5. whose
6. Who's
7. Who's
8. Whose
9. who's
10. who's
11. whose

12. Who's
13. who's
14. Whose
15. who's

**Homonyms:
Exercise 13:
Principal and
Principle (p. 50)**
1. principal
2. Principal
3. principal
4. principle
5. principal
6. principal
7. principle
8. principal
9. principle
10. principal
11. principal
12. principle
13. principal
14. principle
15. principal

**Homonyms:
Exercise 14:
Its and It's (p. 51)**
1. It's
2. it's
3. its
4. its
5. It's
6. its
7. it's
8. it's
9. its
10. its
11. it's
12. its
13. it's
14. it's
15. its

**Homonyms:
Exercise 15:
Their, There, and
They're (p. 52)**
1. They're
2. there
3. they're
4. their
5. There
6. there
7. their

8. they're
9. They're
10. there
11. their
12. they're
13. they're
14. their
15. there

**Homonyms:
Exercise 16:
Stationary and
Stationery (p. 53)**
1. stationery
2. stationery
3. stationary
4. stationary
5. stationery
6. stationary
7. stationary
8. stationary
9. stationary
10. stationery
11. stationery
12. stationary
13. stationary
14. stationary
15. Stationery

**Homonyms:
Exercise 17:
Through and Threw
(p. 54)**
1. threw
2. threw
3. through
4. threw
5. through
6. through
7. threw
8. through
9. through
10. through
11. threw
12. through
13. threw
14. threw
15. through

Homonyms: Exercise 18: Break and Brake (p. 55)
1. brake
2. brake
3. break
4. break
5. break
6. brake
7. brake
8. brake
9. break
10. break
11. break
12. brake
13. break
14. break
15. break

Homonyms: Exercise 19: Cite, Site, and Sight (p. 56)
1. sight
2. sight
3. site
4. sight
5. cite
6. cite
7. site
8. site
9. sight
10. cite
11. sight
12. site
13. sight
14. sight
15. cite

Homonyms: Exercise 20: Review (p. 57)
1. you're
2. Whose
3. sight
4. stationery
5. principal
6. their
7. cite
8. weak
9. stationary
10. who's
11. principle
12. week

13. there
14. site
15. It's
16. your
17. its
18. they're

Homonyms: Exercise 21: Review (p. 58)
1. E
2. U
3. T
4. N
5. O
6. Q
7. G
8. S
9. P
10. K
11. L
12. V
13. W
14. A
15. F
16. R
17. D
18. H
19. C
20. M
21. B
22. I
23. J

Other: Exercise 1: Already and All Ready (p. 64)
1. all ready
2. all ready
3. already
4. all ready
5. already
6. all ready
7. all ready
8. already
9. already
10. all ready
11. all ready
12. already
13. already
14. all ready
15. all ready

Other: Exercise 2: Altogether and All Together (p. 65)
1. all together
2. all together
3. altogether
4. all together
5. altogether
6. all together
7. altogether
8. all together
9. all together
10. altogether
11. all together
12. all together
13. altogether
14. all together
15. all together

Other: Exercise 3: Almost and Most (p. 66)
1. almost
2. Most
3. almost
4. almost
5. most
6. most
7. almost
8. almost
9. most
10. Almost
11. most
12. almost
13. almost
14. most
15. Almost

Other: Exercise 4: Beside and Besides (p. 67)
1. Besides
2. Beside
3. beside
4. Besides
5. besides
6. beside
7. besides
8. beside
9. besides
10. beside
11. besides
12. besides
13. beside
14. beside
15. besides

Other: Exercise 5: Clothes and Cloths (p. 68)
1. clothes
2. clothes
3. cloths
4. clothes
5. cloths
6. cloths
7. clothes
8. cloths
9. clothes
10. clothes
11. cloths
12. clothes
13. clothes
14. clothes
15. cloths

Other: Exercise 6: Desert and Dessert (p. 69)
1. dessert
2. desert
3. dessert
4. dessert
5. desert
6. desert
7. desert
8. dessert
9. desert
10. Desert
11. dessert
12. desert
13. desert
14. dessert
15. desert

Other: Exercise 7: Loose and Lose (p. 70)
1. loose
2. loose
3. lose
4. loose
5. loose
6. lose
7. lose
8. loose
9. loose
10. lose
11. loose
12. lose
13. lose
14. loose
15. lose

Other: Exercise 8: Real and Really (p. 71)
1. real
2. real
3. really
4. really
5. real
6. real
7. really
8. really
9. real
10. real
11. really
12. really
13. really
14. real
15. really

Other: Exercise 9: Review (p. 72)
1. all ready
2. desert
3. loose
4. desert
5. all right
6. besides
7. dessert
8. altogether
9. real
10. beside
11. clothes
12. already
13. most
14. really
15. almost
16. all together
17. desert
18. lose
19. cloths

Other: Exercise 10: Passed and Past (p. 73)
1. past
2. past
3. past
4. passed
5. past
6. past
7. past
8. passed
9. past
10. passed
11. past
12. past

13. past
14. passed
15. past

**Other: Exercise 11:
Quiet and Quite
(p. 74)**
1. quiet
2. quiet
3. quite
4. quite
5. quiet
6. quiet
7. quite
8. quite
9. quiet
10. quite
11. quiet
12. quite
13. quite
14. quiet
15. quiet

**Other: Exercise 12:
Than and Then
(p. 75)**
1. then
2. Then
3. than
4. then
5. then
6. than
7. then
8. then
9. than
10. then
11. than
12. then
13. than
14. than
15. then

**Other: Exercise 13:
Good and Well
(p. 76)**
1. well
2. well
3. good
4. well
5. good
6. well
7. well
8. well
9. well

10. well
11. good
12. good
13. well
14. well
15. good

**Other: Exercise 14:
Bad and Badly
(p. 77)**
1. badly
2. bad
3. bad
4. badly
5. bad
6. badly
7. bad
8. badly
9. bad
10. bad
11. bad
12. badly
13. bad
14. badly
15. badly

**Other: Exercise 15:
Review (p. 78)**
1. bad
2. well
3. quiet
4. dessert
5. desert
6. past
7. then
8. badly
9. passed
10. good
11. quite
12. than
13. well
14. desert
15. past

**Other: Exercise 16:
Accept and Except
(p. 79)**
1. accept
2. except
3. except
4. accept
5. except
6. accept
7. accept

8. except
9. except
10. accept
11. accept
12. accept
13. except
14. Except
15. accept

**Other: Exercise 17:
Bring and Take
(p. 80)**
1. take
2. take
3. take
4. bring
5. Take
6. take
7. bring
8. Bring
9. take
10. bring
11. bring
12. take
13. take
14. take
15. take

**Other: Exercise 18:
Farther and Further
(p. 81)**
1. farther
2. farther
3. Further
4. further
5. farther
6. farther
7. farther
8. further
9. farther
10. further
11. further
12. farther
13. farther
14. farther
15. further

**Other: Exercise 19:
In and Into (p. 82)**
1. into
2. into
3. in
4. in
5. in

6. in
7. into
8. in
9. in
10. into
11. into
12. in
13. into
14. into
15. in

**Other: Exercise 20:
Advice and Advise
(p. 83)**
1. advice
2. advice
3. advise
4. advice
5. advise
6. advise
7. advice
8. advice
9. advise
10. advice
11. advise
12. advise
13. advice
14. advice
15. advice

**Other: Exercise 21:
Review (p. 84)**
1. into
2. advise
3. take
4. farther
5. take
6. accept
7. except
8. farther
9. in
10. advice
11. bring
12. into
13. further
14. in

**Other: Exercise 22:
Review (p. 85)**
1. I
2. G
3. F
4. S
5. J
6. K
7. C
8. A
9. O
10. N
11. B
12. P
13. R
14. Q
15. E
16. H
17. M
18. T
19. D
20. L